MARRIAGE BY THE BOOK

The Secret to Building a Rock-Solid Home

MARRIAGE BY THE BOOK

The Secret to Building a Rock-Solid Home

Dr. Jack Graham

1-800-414-7693 (1-800-414-POWER)
JGRAHAM@POWERPOINT.ORG
JACKGRAHAM.ORG

Published by Dunham Books
Copyright © 2007 by Dr. Jack Graham and
PowerPoint® Ministries
Published 2007

ISBN: 0-9787638-9-0

Cover design by: Ernest+Ideas Design & Media Group

Printed in the United States of America

Marriage by the Book

The Secret to Building a Rock-Solid Home

Dr. Jack Graham

Table of Contents

INTRODUCTION

F or over three decades, God has given me the privilege of being a pastor and minister of the Gospel. And throughout my ministry, I've seen the good, the bad, and the ugly when it comes to marriage, home, and family.

I've seen many wonderful and successful marriages. And my wife, Deb, and I have learned incredible lessons from these godly examples.

But over the years, I have also been called on as a counselor and a friend to work with husbands and wives whose marriages are in trouble. And at times, I've been heartbroken when I've seen marriages...and families...fall apart.

I don't know what shape your marriage is in today, but what I can tell you is this: If you follow God's design, your marriage and your home can be all that you desire...and even more. I know, because it's what Deb and I have experienced in our marriage, our home, and our family since the day we became husband and wife!

Deb and I were married in the small town of Mineral Wells, Texas, on May 22, 1970 (yep, that was a long time ago!). And from the earliest days of our marriage, we applied biblical principles in our life together. While it has not always been without struggle, we have experienced the incredible blessing of God through the years as we have been faithful to make these principles the foundation of our marriage.

We have three children, and today they are all grown and living successful lives, walking with the Lord. And I have to say, it's a wonderful blessing!

So what's the secret? How do you build a marriage and home that can stand against the storms of life? How can *you* have a rock-solid marriage that lasts a lifetime?

By building your marriage according to the blueprint God gives us in His Word.

In the Scripture, God has given us the principles for how to build a marriage that will stand the test of time…principles that produce a marriage that doesn't just survive, but thrives.

You know, there are a number of reasons why marriages

struggle today. One of the greatest reasons is the great confusion that exists about the roles of husbands and wives. Yet God has given us very clear direction for these roles in the Bible.

Another reason many marriages struggle today is because we live in a culture that is quick to run to the divorce court when a marriage isn't "working." Husbands and wives are ready to throw in the towel much too quickly.

For these reasons…and many others…I want to outline for you how to defend your marriage. If you are struggling in your marriage today, it's my prayer that my words of advice and encouragement will put your marriage on the road to healing.

It's also my hope that you will come to understand that the strategy to build a lasting marriage goes beyond your relationship with your spouse. It's also built on your role as the parent of your children. I'm often amazed at the great misunderstanding about parenting in our society today! Far too many homes are run by the children…with great detriment to the marriage and the family.

So I will help give you a biblical perspective on what it

means to be a family in the following pages. And I'll share some very practical advice based on Deb's and my 30-plus years of marriage!

There's no doubt that these are challenging days to build a marriage and raise a family. There are pressures all around us that will tear our homes apart if we're not extremely careful. But by standing on the promises of Scripture, you can stand against those pressures. And as you will see, your marriage… and your family…can thrive in spite of these pressures.

There is a winning strategy to build a rock-solid marriage and home that lasts. It's a *marriage by the Book!*

Chapter 1

A Love that Lasts

It's been said that love at first sight is nothing special. It's when two people have been looking at each other for years that it becomes a miracle!

Deb and I have been "looking at each other" for over 30 years and God has blessed us beyond anything we could have ever imagined! We've worked hard at deepening and strengthening our marriage. But the most important thing we did in the early days of our marriage was to establish our home on biblical fundamentals.

You know, one of the things that is true of every winning team is its commitment to the fundamentals. Executing proper fundamentals is vital if you're going to have a winning team. In fact, every championship sports team majors on the fundamentals. That's why they go to training camp—to get back to the basics. Training camp is all about reinforcing the fundamentals and then learning to apply those fundamentals to game time.

So as we begin our look at what makes for a marriage that lasts, we need to go back to the fundamentals…fundamentals that are found in God's marriage book, the Bible. And if you apply these fundamentals to your marriage, you will begin to build a winning team with your mate. Then your marriage and your family won't just survive during stormy and turbulent times…they will thrive!

God's Desire for You and Your Marriage

The first fundamental of a thriving marriage is having the right mentality. That mentality believes that God does not intend for you to live a miserable life! In John 10:10, Jesus says, "I came that they may have life and have it abundantly." That's not only true for you personally, but it's also true for your marriage! God intends for your marriage to be abundantly blessed.

But if your marriage is going to be blessed, it's going to take some work. It's going to require constant devotion on your part.

I have heard many people say, "My marriage just isn't working anymore." You would think from such a statement that marriage is some sort of a mechanical routine…and that there's something wrong with the marriage institution. Well, the problem is not with the institution—contrary to popular belief. The problem is with the personnel! It's not that marriage "works" or "doesn't work." It's that *we* must work at making our marriage successful.

Some guys spend more time working on their golf game… or working on their car…or working at their job…than they do working on their marriage. As a result, it's an increasing rarity when a marriage stays together for a lifetime…sticking together through thick and thin. Such a flourishing marriage is actually—and sadly—becoming an oddity.

But let me be clear. God wants to bless your marriage. Can I state that again? God *wants* to bless your marriage! But if you are to receive that blessing, you must work at it…and be willing to build your marriage on the fundamentals He outlines in His Word.

Learning from the Author and Founder of Marriage

We often forget who invented marriage and the family. Both are God's idea. Marriage is not a human contract that can be broken at will. It is a divine covenant established by God. It is supreme over all other relationships and it requires complete commitment.

And since God invented marriage, He is the greatest authority on how to build a marriage that will last. He knows better than anyone else the fundamentals required for you to have a marriage that will indeed thrive!

He even put those principles into a book...a marriage manual...that will guide you into the kind of dynamic marriage that you desire. That manual is the Bible.

Now, you may be wondering what the Bible has to say about how you can build a rock-solid marriage in the 21st century. While you might think the Bible is an antiquated piece of history, I can guarantee you it is not! It speaks into our lives today with incredible relevance, revealing the fundamentals of God's strategy for a marriage that will thrive.

As a launching point, I want to take you to the fourth chapter of Ecclesiastes, starting in verse nine:

Two are better than one, because they have a good reward for their toil. For if they fall, one will lift up his fellow. But woe to him who is alone when he falls and has not another to lift him up! Again, if two lie together, they keep warm, but how can one keep warm alone? And though a man might prevail against one who is alone, two will withstand him—a threefold cord is not quickly broken (vv. 9-12).

The first fundamental for building a thriving marriage is to understand that God has designed a "threefold cord" to tie a marriage together. That cord is you, your mate, and the Lord Jesus Christ. If you are to experience the kind of fulfilling, rewarding, and truly strong marriage you desire, it must be tied together by Jesus Christ.

But it starts with you, your spouse, and your commitment to each other. The companionship, partnership, and friendship found in marriage are blessings that so many husbands and wives take for granted. But God makes it clear: "Two are better than one." When you fall, your companion will be there to lift you up. When you lie down together, there's warmth. If there's a problem you are struggling with, the two of you can withstand that problem because there is strength together...especially when you have established your marriage in Jesus Christ.

It's been said that marriage halves our grief and doubles our joy. But for too many couples, marriage is a struggle and full of pain.

In fact, many marriages reflect the saying, "Marriage is like a three-ring circus: an engagement ring, a wedding ring, and suffering." If this kind of circus describes your marriage today, I want you to know you can change. You don't have to have a miserable marriage. You can discover the joy, life, and love that is promised when you do marriage God's way.

I don't believe I've ever met a married person who doesn't desire to have a great marriage. As J. Paul Getty, once known as the richest man in the world, said, "I would give my entire fortune for one happy marriage." How sad! He had everything money could buy...except a happy marriage!

If you have a successful, winning marriage...regardless of how much money you do or don't have in the bank...you are a wealthy person. You have been blessed by God. Because there is nothing on earth...outside of your own personal relationship with Jesus Christ...that is more precious or more valuable than your relationship with your spouse. It is valuable spiritually, emotionally, and physically.

For example, research shows that people who are married live longer than people who are not married. They go to doctors less often and make less use of health care services. Virtually every study I have read regarding mortality and marital status shows that the unmarried of both genders have higher death rates, whether by disease, accident, or suicide.

I have also read the findings from a study that surveyed both married and unmarried men and women to determine which group was the happiest. The happiest group was married men.

Records dating back to the 19th century show that the highest suicide rates occurred among those who were divorced, followed by those who had been widowed and those who had never married. The lowest rates of suicide were among those who were married!

Now, this is not to suggest that if you are single, somehow you are living an inferior life. Not at all! As a matter of fact, God has a plan for every life—including your life. And it could be that God's plan and purpose is for you to serve and glorify Him as a single person. But the fact is that nine out of ten Americans will be married at one point in their life. So if you're not married, I pray this book will help you lay some foundations for your life that prepare you for the future God has for you.

Your Responsibility: To Work on Your Marriage

In July of 1981, the whole world watched as Prince Charles and Lady Diana were married in pomp and circumstance at St. Paul's Cathedral in London. It was a fairytale wedding with 3,500 in attendance and an estimated audience of 750 million people around the world. The people of Britain even enjoyed a national holiday to mark the occasion!

It was a beautiful wedding…a wedding never to be forgotten. But how long did their marriage last? Sadly, it ended up becoming nothing but fodder for the tabloids.

The fact is many people spend more time preparing and working on the wedding day than they do preparing and working on the marriage itself. Some people spend more time building their actual house than they do building a home for Jesus Christ!

Here's my point: Having a strong, winning, healthy marriage is no accident! It doesn't just happen. It is something you have to commit yourself to work on every day. That is your responsibility.

I have often heard people say, "Well, you know, that marriage…it was just made in heaven." I believe marriages are indeed made in heaven. But I also believe that marriages are made on earth.

If you simply say that marriage is made in heaven, you can dodge the responsibility to build your marriage here on earth. You can begin to think that a good marriage is the luck of the draw…and that your marriage may or may not have been made in heaven. You may think that maybe God hasn't blessed your marriage, and therefore, that you need to get out of your marriage and into a marriage that God will bless.

Let me state again that God wants to bless your marriage. It's His plan for your marriage to succeed. But as a husband or wife, you must be willing to put forth the effort that is necessary for you to experience that blessing.

Paul tells us in Philippians 2:12 to "work out your own salvation with fear and trembling." In this verse, he's not telling us to work *for* salvation, but to work *out* our salvation. God gives us the gift of salvation in Jesus Christ, and then we work it out by faith. And as Paul said, we are to do that with fear and trembling.

I believe what is true concerning our salvation is also true of our marriage. Marriage is God's gift to you. And now, as you work it out by spending the energy and effort that is required to build a strong marriage—that's your gift back to God. You must work daily to present your marriage and your family to the glory of God.

This means you must swim against the tide of our culture, when people are more willing than ever to discard their marriage with the idea that maybe they'll do better the next time. Let me be clear and direct: This attitude is not only destroying marriages, but it's destroying families and the very fabric of our society.

Now, we may think this is just the way the world views marriage—that marriage is merely something that is disposable. But what concerns me is this same mentality has crept into the Church of the Lord Jesus Christ. And when you examine the statistics, there's very little difference in the divorce rates for Christians and non-Christians.

The Bible says God hates divorce (Malachi 2:16). Which is why you and I must never condescend to our culture, which leaves the option of divorce open. As followers of Christ, we must raise the standard for marriage up to God's standard! We must understand that divorce is not an option.

As a pastor, I have observed that most marriages are abandoned for no good, biblical reason. And most marriages that end in divorce did not have to end that way.

Yes, there are exceptions that are noted in the Bible. And I will spend some time outlining what the Scripture has to say about divorce later in this book. But even adultery is not grounds for divorce…if you can find restoration and repentance in your life and in your marriage.

I've found that most divorces come about because people give up…because they're just not willing to work at it anymore. They decide to do it their way instead of God's way. Most marriages that fall apart do so because of a lack of obedience to God and a lack of commitment to one another.

It all boils down to one word: *neglect.* I believe the primary culprit in the demise and destruction of marriages today is neglect. Your marriage is like a beautiful garden that must be tended. It must be cultivated. It must be worked on. A great marriage doesn't just happen!

I always chuckle when I hear someone say, "Well, we just fell in love." You don't fall in love, you *grow* in love. And if you're to grow in your love for your spouse, it must be nurtured and cared for like a beautiful garden. You must uproot the weeds and build some fences. And you must realize that it takes both sunshine and rain.

God intends for you to tend to your marriage. And if you

want to have a rock-solid marriage, you can have it. But, again, it's going to take work—and lots of it! That's why God has given us these clear principles in His Word. He wants to show us how to work at marriage so we can build the kind of rock-solid marriage that will last a lifetime.

This is such an important point that I want to give you another illustration.

When you look in a mirror, what do you see? You see a reflection of you. And sometimes it can be frightening and upsetting…especially in the morning! But when you look in the mirror and see your reflection, it's only then that you realize you need some attention…that you need some work!

Well, if you don't like what you see when you look into your marriage mirror, that's not the time to break the mirror and walk away. That's the time to go to work and deal with the problems.

But you must determine to work on your marriage. That's your first decision and the first step in building a rock-solid marriage.

Building the Proper Foundation

Now, once you've made the decision to work on your marriage, you have to make another decision. And that is to build your marriage on a solid foundation.

Every time I stand before a couple to perform their wedding ceremony, I remind them of the story Jesus told of two men who went out to build their houses. The first man built his house on sand, and when the storm came and raged against that house, it collapsed. Great was the fall of that house, because it was built on the sand. It had no foundation.

But the other man built his house upon the rock. And when the storm came—and storms do come in life because the seasons of life change—it stood. It had a solid foundation. The house was built upon the rock and it didn't break apart.

But notice, these two men had a choice. One *chose* to build his house on the sand, and the other *chose* to build his house on the rock. And just like these two men, you must make a choice. You must determine to build your house on a solid foundation. And the only foundation that will stand the storms of life is the Rock of Jesus Christ.

As I mentioned before, we live in a culture that sees marriage as disposable. But the breakdown of marriages and families is a pivotal issue of our day, because as we lose our marriages, we lose our society, our families, and our kids.

The divorce rate has dramatically increased over the past 100 years. For example, the divorce rate in 1900 was about 12% of married couples, but by 2005, it had jumped to 43%— almost one out of every two marriages in the United States. And it's estimated that one million children in America will be negatively affected by divorce this year!

So often divorce is just an excuse for living life independently of God's Word...to walk away from the promise "to love, honor, and cherish as long as we both shall live." Let me remind you that marriage isn't a human contract. It's a divine covenant before God. Human contracts can be broken at will, but in marriage, we make promises to God as well as promises to one another.

In his famous speech to the House of Commons in June of 1940, Winston Churchill made a poignant statement in response to the desire felt by many British citizens to abandon

England when their country was besieged by the Nazis. Churchill said, "Wars are not won by evacuations."

The same is true of marriage! No victory is won by evacuation...by giving up or by quitting. Victory is won by persevering by the grace and the power of God.

As a follower of Christ, you need to determine to keep your marriage from ending up in the divorce court by building it on the solid foundation of Jesus Christ. And that starts by understanding the nature and reason God created the institution of marriage.

The Purpose of Marriage

In Genesis 2:15-25, this is what we read:

Then the LORD God took the man and put him in the garden of Eden to tend and keep it. And the LORD God commanded the man, saying, "Of every tree of the garden you may freely eat; but of the tree of the knowledge of good and evil you shall not eat, for in the day that you eat of it you shall surely die." And the LORD God said, "It is not good that man should be

alone; I will make him a helper comparable to him."
Out of the ground the LORD God formed every beast
of the field and every bird of the air, and brought
them to Adam to see what he would call them. And
whatever Adam called each living creature, that was
its name. So Adam gave names to all cattle, to the
birds of the air, and to every beast of the field. But
for Adam there was not found a helper comparable
to him. And the LORD God caused a deep sleep to
fall on Adam, and he slept; and He took one of his
ribs, and closed up the flesh in its place. Then the rib
which the LORD God had taken from man He made
into a woman, and He brought her to the man. And
Adam said: "This is now bone of my bones and flesh
of my flesh; she shall be called Woman, because she
was taken out of Man." Therefore a man shall leave
his father and mother and be joined to his wife, and
they shall become one flesh. And they were both naked,
the man and his wife, and were not ashamed (NKJV).

Adam had a good life in the Garden of Eden. He

was created by the very hand of God and he spent every day in fellowship and communion with Him. God said that everything in His creation was good. But when He saw the loneliness of man, He said, as recorded in Genesis 2:18, "It is not good that man should be alone; I will make him a helper comparable to him."

So God put Adam to sleep, and out of Adam's rib He created the woman, Eve. God didn't create Eve out of Adam's head so that she would be lord over him or out of his foot so that she would be trampled by him, but out of his rib...near to his side to walk with him, underneath his arm to be protected by him, and near to his heart to be loved by him.

God made the woman as man's "completer," not man's "competitor." In fact, the word *comparable* in verse 18 actually means someone to assist in finding fulfillment. And it is often translated in the Old Testament "to rescue."

God created the woman to rescue the man from his loneliness and emptiness so that he could find fulfillment, satisfaction, and blessing in the companionship of marriage.

Establishing a Rock-Solid Marriage

But how do you establish such a marriage? God shows us in Genesis 2:24 when He says:

Therefore shall a man leave his father and his mother, and shall cleave unto his wife: and they shall be one flesh (KJV).

Now, the word *cleave* in the King James Version of the Bible means to cling, to stick together like glue. So when you get married, all other relationships should change. All lesser ties are to be severed. A man's priority is his relationship with and commitment to his wife. And a wife's priority is her relationship with and commitment to her husband. Yes, we are to honor our parents and respect them, but we are to leave them and establish a new home.

Deb and I got married while we were in college. We were so poor we didn't have two nickels to rub together! But we determined to make it on our own. Even when there was conflict, we worked it out…on our own.

Some couples run to mama the moment there's a little difficulty or there's some financial pressure. Every couple needs to heed God's directive to leave and cleave. You need to work things through and establish your union as husband and wife.

By the way, let me give some advice to in-laws and parents: Hands off, mouths shut, prayers on! If you will do these three things, you will help—not hurt—your children as they work to establish their marriage.

What about friends? What should happen to those relationships when you get married?

Well, it's good to have friends. In fact, friends are vital. But your best friend should be your mate.

No other friendship should take the place of that friendship because a great marriage is built upon a great friendship...not sex...as the world would have you believe. Sure, sex is a vital part of the marriage union, a blessing and gift from God. But a successful marital relationship should first be based on friendship. You must be friends before you are to be lovers.

You know, I've often said that it's one thing to divorce a spouse, but it's almost impossible to divorce your best friend.

Perhaps you've been married a lot of years and have

forgotten what it means to be friends…to take long walks together, to bare your souls and your hearts with each other, to share life together, to just be together. Perhaps you've gone in so many different directions for so many years that you wake up each morning next to a stranger rather than a friend.

Husbands, the Scripture says you are to know your wife and live with your wife in understanding. Do you know your wife? Have you taken the time recently to know her better? Do you know her favorite color? Do you know the color of her eyes? Do you know her favorite food? Do you know her favorite restaurant? Do you know her hopes? Do you know her prayers? Do you know her aspirations? Do you know what she's thinking right now?

A great marriage is made up of two friends…sticking together, fused together, cleaving together.

By the way, the word *cleaving* means determined action. It's a picture of someone climbing a mountain determined to get to the top and hanging on for dear life. And as anyone who's been married for any length of time will tell you, marriage is just like that sometimes! You just have to determine to hang on…no matter how tough of a spot your marriage may be in today.

So determine to work on your marriage. Take responsibility to build it on the Rock of Jesus Christ. Do whatever it takes to strengthen your relationship with your spouse…to make it more wonderful and more beautiful. And get rid of any attitude or ambition or action that is putting distance between the two of you.

Even if the fire of your marriage is ebbing, it can be rekindled in Jesus Christ. Your marriage can burn brightly with the fires of God if you will commit your life to Him and make the choice to rekindle the love, devotion, and commitment you have made to one another.

Chapter 2

The Role of the Husband

In this chapter, I want to talk directly to men. My goal is to help you understand the role God has called you to play as a husband.

You know, it's absolutely critical to have a quarterback on a football team. It's vital to have someone who takes the plays from the coach, communicates the plays to the rest of the team, and then directs and leads the team in the execution of the play.

The same is true for your family. There needs to be a quarterback...someone who is responsible for leading the family.

Now, one of the reasons for so many divorces today is that men and women fail to understand and practice their specific and strategic roles and responsibilities in the marriage. And I believe the bulk of the responsibility for the marriage rests squarely on the shoulders of the man. He is the one called by God to lead his family. He is called to follow Christ and to be God's man for his wife and children. And when this doesn't happen, much damage can be done.

There was a man in the Old Testament by the name of Jonah who got out of the will of God. In fact, he literally ran in the opposite direction from the will of God. He was living in disobedience and almost sunk an entire ship as a result.

Many marriages have been sunk because of the disobedience of a man who has refused to take the responsibility for his marriage. So as a husband, I want to challenge you to take the role God has designed for you.

That role is perhaps best expressed in Ephesians 5:25-33:

Husbands, love your wives, as Christ loved the church and gave himself up for her, that he might sanctify her, having cleansed her by the washing of water with the word, so that he might present the church to himself in splendor, without spot or wrinkle or any such thing, that she might be holy and without blemish. In the same way husbands should love their wives as their own bodies. He who loves his wife loves himself. For no one ever hated his own flesh, but nourishes and cherishes it, just as Christ does the church, because we are members of his body.

"Therefore a man shall leave his father and mother
and hold fast to his wife, and the two shall become
one flesh." This mystery is profound, and I am saying
that it refers to Christ and the church. However, let
each one of you love his wife as himself, and let the
wife see that she respects her husband.

Ephesians chapter 5 talks about the Spirit-filled life. And I believe God intentionally put the direction to husbands in this chapter because the Spirit-filled life is to be applied to the family. While there are a few words given to wives, most of the ink in this passage is given to men because we need it the most. I'm certain of that!

Three words in this passage describe the role and the responsibility the man has in the marriage relationship:

Love...your...wife.

Simple instructions. Husbands, love your wives!

As the man, you hold in your hand the keys to a happy home. God has called you to be the initiator in the relationship with your wife and with your family. And as your wife and children respond to your loving, faithful leadership as a husband and father committed to Christ and committed to them, you will be taking another step in building a rock-solid marriage and family.

That's what it means to love your wife.

Now, I want to give you five ways I believe you are to love your wife:

The first is to **love your wife passionately**.

When I say that you are to love your wife passionately, I'm not talking primarily about sexual love—although the Scripture does say to "let the marriage bed be undefiled" (Hebrews 13:4). Clearly, this is a very important part of the intimacy and relationship between husband and wife in a marriage.

When I say to love your wife passionately, I'm talking about a love that begins in your own heart. It's the kind of love Christ had for the Church when He gave Himself for us.

I truly believe most Christian husbands want to express their love to their wives, but they're just not very good at demonstrating it! Yet Paul says in Ephesians 5:25 that husbands are to love their wives as Christ loved the Church.

And Christ clearly demonstrated His love for us! "But God shows his love for us in that while we were still sinners, Christ died for us" (Romans 5:8).

Now, you're probably thinking, "Hey, I'd be willing to jump in front of a Mack truck for my wife!" But let me ask you another question: Are you willing to die to yourself...to your own ego...and to your own personal ambitions? Are you willing to put your wife first in your life and in your marriage...next to your own relationship with Jesus Christ? That's how you demonstrate your love to your wife.

In the ancient world, there were three words in the Greek language for love. One word was *eros* from which we get the word *erotic*. Eros has to do with sensual or sexual love. But if a marriage is based totally or even primarily upon physical love, then it is sorely lacking in the ultimate kind of passionate love that makes a marriage work. Eros is a lesser kind of love. Again, God has chosen to bless the marriage union with the oneness and the intimacy of the sexual union, but eros is not the best kind of love.

Another word for love in the Scripture is *philo*. It

means brotherly love, and it's the word from which we get our word *Philadelphia*. It's the love of family and the love of friends, or the love of compatibility. "I love you because you're like me." It's the love that is conditioned upon friendship or a relationship.

But there's another kind of a love, a love the Bible describes as the highest kind of love of all. It's *agape* love. This love is the giving love of Jesus Christ and is used in John 3:16, "For God so loved the world, that he gave his only Son, that whoever believes in him should not perish but have eternal life." In the love of Jesus Christ, we have the perfect and pure example of the kind of love that we as husbands are to give to our wives. That is truly passionate love!

Some men get into marriage for the same reason a tick gets on a dog: to see what he can get out of it. But what makes a great marriage is not what you *get*, but what you *give*. As husbands, we need to be like Jesus, who completely gave Himself away for us.

In Philippians 2:5-11, Paul gives us incredible insight into what agape love really looks like:

*Have this mind among yourselves, which is yours
in Christ Jesus, who, though he was in the form of
God, did not count equality with God a thing to be
grasped, but made himself nothing, taking the form
of a servant, being born in the likeness of men. And
being found in human form, he humbled himself by
becoming obedient to the point of death, even death
on a cross. Therefore God has highly exalted him and
bestowed on him the name that is above every name,
so that at the name of Jesus every knee should bow, in
heaven and on earth and under the earth, and every
tongue confess that Jesus Christ is Lord, to the glory
of God the Father.*

When Paul says that Jesus "made himself nothing," it
literally means Jesus emptied Himself. Jesus loved us by
emptying Himself. Now, He didn't empty Himself of His deity,
as He never once ceased to be totally God. In His humanity…
in His flesh…His deity was veiled, but it was never voided.

Even though Jesus was totally God, He chose to be a
servant. As he said in Mark 10:45, "For even the Son of

Man came not to be served but to serve, and to give his life as a ransom for many." He came to die for us! And here's the paradox of spiritual authority. Because Jesus humbled Himself...because He gave Himself...because He offered and sacrificed Himself...the Father now has exalted Him as King of kings and Lord of lords.

This is also the paradox of marriage. By emptying yourself as husband and by choosing to serve your wife, you will love her and lead her as God desires. And then He will exalt you! As 1 Peter 5:6 reminds us, "Humble yourselves, therefore, under the mighty hand of God so that at the proper time he may exalt you."

When most men marry, they think that they fulfill their role as a husband by throwing their weight around and by bullying their wife and family. For some husbands, their favorite verse is "Wives, submit to your husbands" (Colossians 3:18). But if you think that the love, respect, response, and submission of your wife will come as a result of you demanding it, you are very, very mistaken.

Your wife will respond to you in love, respect, and

honor when you are willing to lead her as a servant…when you love her passionately with the love of Jesus Christ both symbolically and in substance.

Now, the symbol of power in most marriages is the remote control. And I'll admit that I'm in charge of the remote control in our house. Like most men, I'm a channel surfer! When Deb and I watch TV, I like to flip from channel to channel during commercial breaks.

Every once in a while, though, Deb will take the remote control and just park on a channel. It drives me nuts, because like most women, she'll settle on a program and watch it for a long time. And I want to be flipping from channel to channel!

But to be the servant leader that Christ has called us to be, we have to be willing to give up even something as simple as the remote control when it is a symbol of authority. When you give it up, it sends your wife the message that she is more important than you, and that you are willing to empty yourself of your agenda.

If you've never done something as simple as giving your wife the remote control, try it some time. You'll send a very simple, but powerful message of your willingness to serve her. But be ready for her to faint when you do it!

So are you willing to die a little bit every day to your own personal whims, wishes, ambitions, and attitudes? Are you willing to put your wife first in your marriage? If you do, you will love her passionately!

The second way to love your wife is to **love your wife with a pure love**.

The love of Jesus Christ is a pure love. In Ephesians 5:26-27, Paul tells us that Christ gave His life "that he might sanctify her, having cleansed her by the washing of water with the word, so that he might present the church to himself in splendor, without spot or wrinkle or any such thing, that she might be holy and without blemish."

Jesus' pure love is an unconditional love! He loves us without condition. It's not based on how we respond to it. And husbands, this is the kind of love we are to express to our wives! This is the kind of love that lasts because it is a committed love...a constant love. It means that as a husband, we're not simply promise makers, we're promise keepers.

By the way, I pray that you meant it when you stood at the altar and promised, "Till death do us part." And I trust by the power of God, you're keeping the vows that you made...that you're faithful, true, and pure!

I told Deb a long time ago, "Honey, if you ever leave me, I'm going with you." We're together for life. That's a pure and lasting love!

The third way to love your wife is to **love your wife with a purposeful love**.

What do I mean by a "purposeful" love? It's captured in Ephesians 5:26, a verse we looked at earlier. It tells us we are to sanctify our wives...to cleanse our wives.

Now, you may be thinking, "What on earth does that mean?" It means you are to take the spiritual assignment from God to lead your wife. To lead her to know, to love, and to follow Jesus Christ.

You may feel like your wife won't change. Even if you believe that's true, you need to love her with the unconditional, *purposeful* love of Christ. If you do, you will begin to see Jesus Christ changing her from the inside out!

Your assignment as a husband is to present your bride to Christ, with the goal that all the beauty and the love of Christ will shine through her.

I believe you can tell the character and faith of a man by the countenance of his wife, because his wife is a reflection of his walk with God. Your wife should be a stronger Christian… a better Christian…because of your walk with God and how you lead her.

What is it about men that makes us so hesitant to even pray with our wives? Is it because we don't want to open up? Is it because we're not willing to share our own spiritual heart with them…our defeats as well as our victories? Whatever the case may be, I encourage you to pray with your wife. Be the spiritual leader God has called you to be by purposefully loving your wife!

The fourth way to love your wife is to **love your wife with a protective love**.

Once you have focused on helping your wife love and live for the Lord, you need to make sure that you are providing your wife the security she needs.

The Bible says in 1 Peter 3:7, "Likewise, husbands, live with your wives in an understanding way, showing honor to the woman as the weaker vessel, since they are heirs with you of the grace of life, so that your prayers may not be hindered."

What does it mean when it says "showing honor to the woman as the weaker vessel"? Does it mean that your wife is somehow inferior? Absolutely not! The "weaker vessel" means that she is the more precious vessel.

This verse is not saying that your wife is somehow inferior, but rather that you are to honor your wife by giving her a position as one who is treasured…to treat her as an "heir with you of the grace of life." That is a protective love.

And this protective love means you are providing and protecting her emotionally, physically, and materially.

The fifth and final way you are to love your wife is to **love your wife with a providing love**.

This kind of love means you are providing your wife with the emotional strength, stability, security, and spiritual leadership that she needs. How do you do that? I believe it starts with kindness. Paul said in 1 Corinthians 13:4 that love is kind. So try giving your wife a little tenderness!

I know we're supposed to be tough and macho men. But true love is tender. In fact, the love of Jesus Christ, which is the strongest love in the universe, is the most tender love. So try a little tenderness. There's power in that kind of love.

A while back a group of German researchers was looking for the secret to living a long and successful life. Their research made a surprising discovery: The secret to the longevity of life is kissing your wife!

The German researchers discovered that men who kiss their wives each morning had fewer automobile accidents on the way to work. And they missed fewer days of work and made more money than non-kissers!

I don't know if kissing your wife each morning will make you healthier, but I promise it will make your marriage healthier. If you show this kindness and love to your wife each day, it can't help but have a positive impact.

Tender love is also shown by opening the door and pulling out the chair. That's a love that is a providing love.

You also love your wife with a providing love through

communication. Research shows that women speak an average of 50,000 words a day, with some blowing gusts of up to 100,000 words or more! But the average man speaks 25,000 words a day…24,999 of which have been used up when men get home from work!

But as a husband, you have to be willing to communicate by opening your heart and life…to listen and to be there for your wife. That means that when you're home, you're really there.

Now, communication between men and women is difficult because we are so different. For example:

- When she says, "Let's ask for directions," he hears, "You're not a man."
- When she asks, "May I have the remote control?" he hears, "Oh, yeah, let's watch something that will bore us all to tears!"
- When she says, "Honey, you need to get in touch with your inner feelings," he hears, "Blah, blah, blah, blah, blah, blah, blah!"
- When she asks, "Are you listening to me?" he hears,

"Blah, blah, blah, blah, blah, blah, blah!"

- When she says, "I'd like to redecorate the house," he hears, "Let's just take our money and flush it down the toilet!"

We end up with a failure to communicate! This is something you have to really work on if you are committed to love your wife with a providing love!

It's easy to think that you can't do all this. But let me encourage you by saying that it's not natural for any one of us to love like this. It's supernatural. This kind of love can only be expressed through a Spirit-filled life. You can't love like this, but Jesus can love like this *through* you.

If you are truly committed to love your wife as Christ has commanded you to love her, you need to pray and ask the Spirit of the living Christ to fill you every day…that you may be emptied of self so that the supernatural power of God's love and grace will fill you. It's only through the work of the Spirit of Jesus in you that you will be able to love like this. You can't do it on your own.

I challenge you today to follow hard after Him with

all your heart. By God's power and by God's grace, be the spiritual leader and steadfast lover in your marriage, home, and family.

CHAPTER 3

The Role of the Wife

To build a rock-solid marriage and home, it's vital for the woman to understand the role and responsibility God has given her in marriage. This is especially true today, as there is such vast misunderstanding...and even ignorance...regarding the position and role of women in the home.

Those of us who are evangelical, Bible-believing Christians are often portrayed and perceived as being anti-woman and archaic in our position regarding the role of women in marriage and the home. A great example of this misconstrued perception is found in a statement from Olga Vives, vice president for the National Organization of Women (NOW), who openly attacked the Promise Keepers organization.

Ms. Vives stated, "This organization breeds bigots. Underneath the façade of Christian religion are the workings of the radical religious right, mobilizing men against the rights of women...Let's remember they blame women's equality for society's ills."

While this is the view of radical feminism, it is unfortunately also the view of some Christians today. There is great confusion in the Church regarding the role of women in society, in the church, and certainly in the home.

The lines...the distinctives...between men and women are more deluded and blurred than ever before. Radical feminism has distorted the distinctiveness between masculinity and femininity. And as a result, the foundations of our social structures are shaking.

A part of this confusion comes from the growth and acceptance in our society—and our world—of the homosexual movement. It's a movement that insists that the homosexual lifestyle is quite normal, and that it's even healthy and good. This perspective is being promoted daily in the popular media. As a result, a growing number of youth are at a crisis point.

Any kind of movement that distorts the distinctiveness between men and women as God created them is ultimately destructive to both men *and* women...and society at large.

So what does the Bible truly say about the role and responsibilities of women? Well, first, you have to remember that the Christian faith is a radical and revolutionary movement. It has been and always will be counter-cultural. When the writers of the New Testament—inspired by the Holy Spirit—gave us God's position on the role of women, it was absolutely counter-cultural...and life-changing!

In that day, women were perceived and treated as chattel, as possessions that could be discarded at will. But when Jesus came along, He elevated the role and the position of womanhood...as did Paul, Peter, and the other writers of the New Testament.

And today's way of looking at marriage and the woman's role in the marriage relationship is not working either...especially when almost one out of two marriages ends in divorce!

But when a marriage is built on God's principles and in His way, it works! In fact, research shows that a Christian couple who prays together, reads the Bible together, and attends church regularly has a divorce rate of only 1 in 1,105!

So what does God have to say about the role of women in marriage? I believe one of the clearest pictures is painted in 1 Peter 3:1-7. In this passage, we find a text that is shocking to some, but absolutely beautiful and wonderful to those who know and love their Bibles:

> *Likewise, wives, be subject to your own husbands, so that even if some do not obey the word, they may be won without a word by the conduct of their wives—when they see your respectful and pure conduct. Do not let your adorning be external—the braiding of hair, the wearing of gold, or the putting on of clothing—but let your adorning be the hidden person of the heart with the imperishable beauty of a gentle and quiet spirit, which in God's sight is very precious. For this is how the holy women who hoped in God used to adorn themselves, by submitting to their husbands, as Sarah obeyed Abraham, calling him lord. And you are her children, if you do good and do not fear anything that is frightening. Likewise, husbands, live with your wives in an understanding way, showing honor to the woman as the weaker*

vessel, since they are heirs with you of the grace of life, so that your prayers may not be hindered.

The first thing I want to focus on is the issue of submission...which may be one of the most misunderstood concepts in the Church today.

The idea of submission, according to the Scripture, is always in the context of mutual submission. This mutual submission is between husbands and wives, as well as Christians toward one another.

You see, submission is not just for wives. Submission is for Christians. We're told clearly in the Word of God that we're to submit to one another (Ephesians 5:21), because submission is yielding our rights for the benefit of others.

And in marriage, submission doesn't begin with the woman. It begins with a husband who lovingly leads his wife. As Christ loves the Church, so husbands are to love their wives.

Now, can you think of any greater act of submission in the history of the world than when Christ submitted Himself to die in agony upon the cross for the sins of the world? He denied His own rights and freely went to the cross to pay for our sins! That's the kind of love that a husband is to have towards his wife...sacrificially loving and leading her in the bonds and beauty of Christian commitment.

When a husband loves his wife in this way, the natural response of the wife is to love her husband. It's the same kind of response we have to Christ and His great love for us. We love Him because He first loved us. And we're able to love, worship, follow, and yes, submit to Him because we know how greatly we've been loved.

So when a husband loves his wife sacrificially, unconditionally, and unreservedly, as Christ loves the Church, then a wife can respond in love because she knows she is truly loved.

But unfortunately, this kind of love is not man's natural inclination. In fact, the natural inclination is to live for self. And it has created a tension in marriage and between the sexes.

This tension has its roots back in the Garden of Eden with Adam and Eve. Through their rebellion and sinful choice, they determined to go their way rather than God's way. And as a result, the curse of sin was placed upon mankind. When God explained the consequences of their sin, He had a particular word to the woman. He said, "Eve, it's going to be very different for you and Adam now."

We find the specifics in the last portion of Genesis 3:16. It's a phrase that is extremely relevant to the issue of how a man and woman relate. It says, "Your desire shall be for your husband, and he shall rule over you."

The word *desire* in this phrase is a very interesting Hebrew word. It literally means to compel or to control. God was letting Eve know...and every woman who would come after her...that she would now have a selfish inclination to control and compel her husband. Just as Adam—due to the selfishness of sin that was born in him—had the desire to rule and dominate his wife, Eve also had a bent to control and compel her husband.

And today, we live with the implications of that curse in our marriages. There is a sin-born inclination for both man and woman to control the other. Because of the sinfulness of men and women, as the sons of Adam and the daughters of Eve, we're all born with an inclination that says, "I'm going to live for me now." And the way that inclination is expressed in marriage is for the husband to have a desire to control, dominate, and rule over his wife and for the wife to want to compel and control her husband.

This bent towards self-focus is apparent in many homes today. Husbands and wives are living for self rather than submitting to God's plan and God's way of submission. And the only antidote for this is to heed the command of Scripture, which says to mutually submit to one another. This means for a man to love his wife and to express that love...the willingness to submit to and sacrifice for her. He must be willing to die for her. For a wife, this means responding to her husband in the same manner, denying self and submitting to him.

And because marriage is a journey and not a destination, this is something both husbands and wives have to do every day. We must constantly die to ourselves and our own selfish desires if our marriages are to thrive, because those selfish desires will always seek to control us.

One of the reasons this is such a significant issue for women is that somehow men have gotten the notion that they are to rule over their wives. The problem is the Bible never commands a man to rule over his wife. The only thing the Bible commands a husband to do is to love his wife!

In addition, the Bible does not teach submission of women to men in society at large. The concept of submission is always in the context of the family. We find throughout Scripture that women were judges, rulers, prophets, and business leaders. There is just no biblical basis for believing that somehow a man is superior to a woman.

So the issue of submission isn't about superiority or inferiority...it has to do with the role and the responsibility of a husband and a wife in the marriage relationship. Submission is not about a woman being a doormat or being dominated and controlled by her husband. Instead it is something God requires of both husband and wife.

Just as we love and respond to Christ in submission, we're to submit to one another.

What a Husband Needs from His Wife

So if submission is something that God requires of both

the husband and wife, what can a wife do to meet the needs of her husband?

A husband needs a wife who respects him, regards him, honors him, prefers him, notices him, esteems him, and believes in him. And what he doesn't need is a wife who disrespects him by being insulting, critical, non-supportive, and passive toward meeting his needs. God created the wife to be the helper...the completer...of her husband. Both husband and wife can become far more together than they could have ever been apart from their relationship.

I love the story of Pete Flattery and his wife, Nancy. Pete was the mayor of Pittsburgh at one time, and he and Nancy were surveying a city construction project one day. As they were walking around the project, one of the construction workers recognized Nancy and said, "Hey, Nancy, remember me? We went to high school together. In fact, we used to date each other!" Immediately Nancy recognized her old friend. They exchanged pleasantries for a few minutes and then she walked on.

As she and Pete walked away, he started teasing her just

a little bit and said, "Well, imagine that. Had you married that man, you would have been married to a construction worker!" And Nancy responded with a smile, "No...if I had married him, I would have been married to the mayor of Pittsburgh!"

Men need someone to believe in them, to encourage them, and to help them be all that God has designed them to be.

The wife who lovingly submits herself to her husband like this is such an incredible asset to him. How I thank God for Deb, my wife, who has been willing to walk by my side through the years...and sometimes stood aside...that I might do and be what God has called me to. As I look back, I believe she has fulfilled a role and an assignment in life that, in my opinion, is far greater than the role and assignment I have had.

A Deeper Understanding of Submission

To submit literally means to rank under. It's a term used to describe the various ranks within the military. It is intended to define the role, not the quality, of the individual. A general isn't necessarily a better man than a sergeant. But there needs to be a definition of the rank in order to define the role each is to fulfill.

This is also true on an athletic team. Every team needs a coach. And as my friend Adrian Rogers once said, "Anything without a head is dead, and anything with two heads is a freak!" And unfortunately, we've got a lot of dead marriages today with no leadership…and too many freakish marriages with two heads!

But there is another way to understand submission—in its meaning "to make an offer." For instance, if you submit something in conversation, you are making an offer. If you submit a contract to someone, let's say a real estate deal, for example, you are submitting your resources to make the deal.

Submission is not just a way to define roles, it is offering of oneself to another. And in looking at the role of the wife, I believe submitting to your husband is to offer yourself and your resources to him. This is vital to making a marriage work.

Are Women Inferior to Men?

Most people believe that submission is an admission of inferiority. Let me make it clear again, women are not inferior to men. In fact, women are far superior to men…at being women. And men are far superior to women…at being men! That's just the way God made us.

So when the Bible talks about submission, it is not a matter of inferiority.

Let me point you to a passage that will help you understand this truth in a clear and powerful way. It's 1 Corinthians 11:3, where Paul states this:

But I want you to understand that the head of every man is Christ, the head of a wife is her husband, and the head of Christ is God.

What? The head of Christ is God? You may be thinking, "I thought the Bible teaches that Jesus is God…that He is co-equal, co-eternal with God. Didn't Jesus say, 'I and the Father are One?' So how could God be the head of Christ?"

Obviously, it doesn't mean that God the Father is superior to God the Son, or that God the Son is inferior to God the Father. Rather, in 1 Corinthians 11, Paul is speaking of God the Son humbling Himself in His humanity as He submitted His will to the will and the plan of the heavenly Father.

Jesus is totally equal with God. But in the divine design of His deity, God the Son submitted Himself to the Father. It's not an issue of inferiority, but of coming under the leadership of the Father.

So when it says that the man is the head of the wife as God is the head of Christ, it does not imply or suggest that a woman is inferior to a superior man. Instead, it is pointing to the relationship within the role and the context of a committed Christian marriage…that the wife is to submit to the leadership and the headship of her husband.

This certainly doesn't mean that a wife is just supposed to sit down and shut up until she's spoken to. When I look back over our marriage, Deb and I have shared in all the major decisions…and in most of the minor decisions. In fact, I can't think of a decision that we've made that we've not made together. How I value Deb's input and her influence!

Submission Starts with a Proper Attitude

If you're going to submit to your husband as God has commanded, it starts with a proper attitude. It's not an attitude that says, "I'm going to submit to this guy even if it kills me!" Instead, it's a joyful spirit that says, "I love God, I love my husband, and I love my family. And I'm going to live my life God's way and not my way."

This is beautifully illustrated in 1 Peter 3:1-2, where it says:

Likewise, wives, be subject to your own husbands,
so that even if some do not obey the word, they may
be won without a word by the conduct of their wives—
when they see your respectful and pure conduct.

This is a critical passage as it reminds us that submission starts with an attitude that is unwavering in its commitment... even if the marriage isn't ideal. Peter doesn't give a pass to a woman whose husband is not a strong Christian or a believer. Instead, Peter commands a believing woman who is married to an unbeliever not to leave him...and not to lecture him. But rather, she is to love that unbelieving or disobedient husband so that by her life and by her love, he might be brought to Christ.

If your husband is an unbeliever, don't try to nag him into the Kingdom of God by putting little Gospel tracts in his briefcase on his way to work or by quoting Scripture at him constantly. Just love your husband, live for Christ, and let him see the difference that Jesus makes in your life. And by the grace of God he may join you in the faith!

1 Peter 3 goes on to tell us what this attitude of submission should look like:

> *Do not let your adorning be external—the braiding of hair, the wearing of gold, or the putting on of clothing—but let your adorning be the hidden person of the heart with the imperishable beauty of a gentle and quiet spirit, which in God's sight is very precious* (v. 3-4).

True submission radiates from the heart and expresses itself in a kind of beauty that shines through a woman's life. True submission means that you don't major on the externals... which is hard not to do in our society today!

Now, I'm not suggesting...nor is this passage suggesting...that a woman should neglect her physical appearance. Instead, it is setting a different standard...that a woman is to concentrate on her inner beauty more than her outer beauty. It's what Proverbs 31:30 is talking about when it says, "Charm is deceitful, and beauty is vain, but a woman who fears the LORD is to be praised."

Beauty consultants will tell you that no matter how physically attractive a woman may be on the outside, she will never look beautiful if she's filled with negative things like anger or anxiety or depression or disillusionment or lack of fulfillment...no matter what they do to her on the outside.

But on the other hand, you can take a woman who's rather plain, yet glowing with the goodness of God, the gentleness of the Holy Spirit, and the presence of Jesus in her life, and she will be a beautiful display of what God can do in a woman's life. That's real cosmetics!

And how does this beauty express itself? It expresses itself in a gentle and quiet spirit. It doesn't mean mousy. It's not talking about whether you're an extrovert or an introvert. What 1 Peter 3:3-4 points to is the attitude of gentleness and teachability...a willingness to respond, learn, and to listen. That is true beauty!

In verses 5 and 6 of 1 Peter 4, we are given an example of what such an attitude looks like:

For this is how the holy women who hoped in God used to adorn themselves, by submitting to their husbands, as Sarah obeyed Abraham, calling him lord. And you are her children, if you do good and do not fear anything that is frightening.

Now don't think that Sarah was some sort of mousy woman. In Genesis, we read that when she and Abraham followed God's command and went to Egypt, Abraham was scared to death he was going to lose her to Pharaoh's harem... and she was 65 at the time!

You see, it was common in those days for a pharaoh to kill a man and take his wife. So Abraham, afraid for his own life, told Pharaoh that Sarah...this good-looking woman with him...was his sister!

And what's even more remarkable, 25 years later when Sarah was nearly 90, she and Abraham went into the land of the Philistines and Abraham did the same thing because Abraham was afraid that the Philistine king was going to take his wife.

Now, I'm certain that the years had done a number on

Sarah, but there was something about the inner quality and the inner beauty of her life...her faithfulness to God and the faithfulness of her life to her husband...that radiated with the glory and the presence of God. As a result, she shone with the beauty that could only be attributed as the beauty of Jesus in her. And when she died at age 127, her husband Abraham wept for days and months and years because he had lost a faithful, loving wife who had walked with him and encouraged him and blessed him for so long.

You know, there's a story of a kite that was soaring high in the sky. And the kite looked over in the distance and saw a beautiful field of flowers. And so the kite said to itself, "I want to fly over there and take a closer look at all those beautiful flowers in the field." But there was a problem because the kite couldn't go that far. The kite was on a string.

So the little kite jerked and pulled and tussled and wrestled with that string until finally the kite broke free. And you know what happened? The wind took it down and it crashed far short of the field. What was holding the kite...the string...was actually elevating and enabling the kite to fly.

Now to me, the string on that kite symbolizes God's plan for your marriage, including submission. And as the winds of the Spirit of God blow through your life in a lifting and loving environment, as a godly Christian woman you will be enabled to soar in the heavenlies. God made you as a woman and a wife to soar and to experience life in the fullest. So don't look at the string of submission as something that's prohibitive. Look at it as a protective way for you to grow as a joint heir of Jesus Christ.

As you think through your role as wife to your husband, I challenge you to ask yourself three questions:

1. Am I willing to put my husband's needs above my own?

2. Am I willing to make whatever sacrifice is necessary in order for my marriage to be everything God intends for it to be?

3. Am I willing—without reservation—to do what the Scripture says regarding my role and responsibility in my marriage?

Philippians 4:13 says, "I can do all things through Him who strengthens me." You can't do any of this without the power of the Holy Spirit...or without putting Christ at the center of your heart and life. But as you do, He will give you the power to be the wife you truly want to be. He'll help you be able to say from your heart, "Honey, I will love you. Honey, I will respect and honor you. Honey, I will believe in you as long as we both shall live."

CHAPTER 4

The Role of the Child

George Bush, former president of the United States, was once asked in an interview, "What do you consider your most important achievement in life?" Now, he could have looked back over an exemplary career and cited many things.

In World War II, he was a war hero. Then he became an elected official, and was later appointed head of the CIA. At one point, he was the ambassador to China. And then, of course, he served two terms as vice president of the United States under Reagan, and then was president of the United States. As president, he led us through Desert Storm and beat back the assault and the tyranny of Saddam Hussein against Kuwait.

There were many things in George Bush's life that he could have pointed to as his most important achievement. And yet, he said: "The proudest thing...is that my children come home."

I would say that this is a man who has his priorities in order, a man who understands that his most important role in life is not as the head of the CIA, or as an ambassador, or even as president of the United States. He understands that his most important role in life is being a dad.

When we get to the end of our lives, we're not going to look back and remember the accolades and the applause we received as a result of our achievements or our success in business. We'll remember how we were as parents. The legacy we leave will be the legacy of our children. That is our *lasting* legacy.

Since the '60s, there have been efforts to redefine the family...efforts that continue to this day. But not too long ago, there was a Harvard research study that examined the lives of children from ages 5 and 6 through their teenage years. The goal of the study was to understand what makes a child successful in life and what makes a child a juvenile delinquent. What they discovered in this Harvard study is that kids who were successful in life had fathers who were firm and fair with discipline, mothers who supervised them and were present in their lives, parents who had affection for one another, and families who spent time together.

After reading this venerable Harvard research, I had just one thing to say: "Duh!"

It doesn't take a Harvard researcher to tell us how significant the family is to raising children. It's critical for moms and dads to fulfill their roles as husbands and wives loving one another…and as parents, providing an atmosphere of nurturing care for their children.

Now, you may be wondering why I'm addressing the issue of parenting in a book on marriage. Well, one of the greatest and most important things you will ever do as husband and wife is to be a dad and mom. To raise children who will someday follow after God with all their hearts.

So in this chapter, I want to address your role as parents. And I want to do this by looking at Psalm 127:3-5, which says the following:

> *Behold, children are a heritage from the LORD,*
> *the fruit of the womb a reward. Like arrows in the*
> *hand of a warrior are the children of one's youth.*

Blessed is the man who fills his quiver with them! He shall not be put to shame when he speaks with his enemies in the gate.

The Gift of Children

I know there are husbands and wives who have been unable to have children. Some have adopted children and others have not. I want you to know that I understand your situation.

But in this chapter, I want to deal directly with husbands and wives to whom God has given children because it is vital for parents to have a proper perspective and appreciation for what God has given them. In fact, our passage says, "Behold, children are a heritage from the LORD, the fruit of the womb a reward."

One of the first things parents need to do is embrace the fact that children are an incredible reward from God. Mom and Dad, your son(s) or daughter(s) are not a burden, but a blessing. In fact, the word translated *heritage* in this passage is actually the word *gift*. You need to see your children as gifts from God.

Now, because your children are gifts from God, the proper perspective is to see them as on loan to you. Which means you are not an owner of your children, but a steward. And as a steward, it is your responsibility to raise your children to become dependent upon the Lord Jesus Christ—not on you.

The Challenge of Right Priorities

In Psalm 127:2, the psalmist highlights a problem that we all face. It says:

It is in vain that you rise up early and go late to rest, eating the bread of anxious toil; for he gives to his beloved sleep.

I believe this is a description of the fast-paced lifestyle that many of us are living today. There's no doubt that ours is a stress-filled generation.

USA Today published an article once in which they focused on the "good life." They examined the good life today compared to the good life a generation ago. Interestingly enough, our parents and grandparents had very basic necessities and very few luxuries, and yet they found their lives very satisfying and very happy.

By contrast, today's generation requires a lot more to be happy and to feel like we are living the good life. Our parents' generation needed just one black-and-white television. Now we need an HDTV…in every room! Our parents' generation was happy to have a car. Now we need nice cars…and everybody who can drive in the family needs one! Our parents' generation was happy just to take a road trip for vacation, but now, we have to travel to luxury locations. And it's not enough to have just one house, we now need a vacation house!

Now, of course, there's nothing wrong with these things if God gives them to you. But if you make these things the criteria for the good life and you work overtime and sacrifice your family to try and obtain them, you will end up sorely disappointed. That's why the psalmist warned us that it's vain to rise up early, to stay up late, and to endure sleepless nights just trying to live the good life!

Why? Because the good life is right in your home…right in your heart. And it begins with your children.

One father, in looking back over his life, gave us this powerful word:

If I had it to do all over again, I would love my wife more in front of my children. I would laugh more with my children at our mistakes and joys. I would listen more…even to the smallest child. I would be more honest about my own weaknesses and stop pretending perfection. I would pray differently for my family: Instead of focusing on them, I'd focus on me and my walk with God. I would do more things together with my children. I would provide more encouragement and bestow more praise. I would pay more attention to little things…deeds and words of love and kindness. And then finally, if I had it to do all over again, I would share God more intimately with my family. In every ordinary thing that happened in every ordinary day, I would direct them to God.

The Absent Father Syndrome

One of the problems in our society today, and particularly

in America, is the absent father. These are fathers who are missing in action. If you talk to children, you will find many who will say, "My dad doesn't take time for me," or "My dad doesn't take me anywhere," or "My dad doesn't talk to me." And too often, the last person children go to is their dad because they don't know them very well.

Some men will talk about how they spend quality time with their kids. But quality time is a myth! Kids don't know the difference between time and quality time...they just know time!

This is a serious issue for fathers today. In fact, the average father in America spends just eight minutes a day with his children on a weekday. Just eight minutes! And on weekends, it's only 14 minutes!

Most men will protest by saying, "I'm too busy...I've got a lot going on." If that's your excuse, I challenge you to examine your priorities because the fact is you can have more free time if that's your goal. The problem is most men are spending their free time doing their own thing rather than spending their free time with their families! You can change your life and you can change your lifestyle if you choose.

Don't be like the dad I quoted earlier. You never want to have to be in the place where you wonder what might have been if only you had spent more time with your kids.

One fellow by the name of David...a dad...wrote these words to Dr. Laura, the radio counselor:

How many?

How many nights do I have, God?

How many nights do I have to tuck each of my boys into bed with their teddy bears?

How many times do I have left, God?

How many times do I have left to lift my boys up onto my shoulders before they're too big?

How many more kisses, God?

How many more kisses do I get to give to my boys after I've tucked them in at night?

How many pushes, God?

How many pushes do I get to give my boys on a swing before they outgrow it?

How many days, God?

*How many days of hot summer do I have left
to run through the sprinklers with my boys?*

How many more tears, God?

*How many more tears of joy will I shed at the end of each day
that my boys have grown through?*

How many more times, God?

*How many more times will I get to lift my boys back into bed
once they've fallen out?*

How many more years, God?

*How many more years before they come and lift me from the
floor after I've fallen?*

How many, God? How many?

Dads, the question of how many is up to you if you hold those children in your hands right now. How many?

Where Are You Aiming Your Kids?

As a parent, you have an incredible opportunity to aim your kids into the future. In Psalm 127:4, the psalmist goes on to say that children are "like arrows in the hand of a warrior." An arrow is to be launched against the enemy. And you have a choice as a parent to *not* give your children over to today's culture, but rather to launch them in love to change our world and culture.

Have you ever noticed that an arrow can go where the warrior cannot go? And your children will go to a time and a place that you will never go. But just like arrows, they must be aimed in the right direction. That is the high and holy responsibility and opportunity you have as parents.

Now, Mark Twain must have known what it was to raise children, especially teenagers. Several generations ago he said, "When your child turns 13, get a barrel, take off the lid, drill some holes in it, put him in the barrel and feed him through the knotholes." And then he said, "When the child turns 16, plug up the knotholes!"

Well, Moses had better advice than Mark Twain. It's advice that is just as relevant today as when he stated it. He says in Deuteronomy 6:4-7:

"Hear, O Israel: The LORD our God, the LORD is one. You shall love the LORD your God with all your heart and with all your soul and with all your might. And these words that I command you today

shall be on your heart. You shall teach them diligently to your children, and shall talk of them when you sit in your house, and when you walk by the way, and when you lie down, and when you rise."

The way to aim your children in the right direction and send them into the future is within the context of a loving family. It's not done by spouting and preaching sermons, but rather spending time living out biblical principles in your life. Your kids need a model and they need a mentor. They need a model to give them an example and a mentor to train them and develop them.

And that's exactly what this passage is talking about when it speaks of teaching these principles. They are to be a fundamental part of your lifestyle…when you get up, when you lay down, when you walk through the day, and when you sit down at the table. In other words, the best way to teach and train your children is in the atmosphere and environment of a home that consistently lives out the principles of a godly life.

The natural, spontaneous, spiritual development of your child will flow from your heart as a parent who loves God.

That's why it says in verse 6 of this passage, "these words that I command you today *shall be on your heart*" (italics added). When the love of God…when the passion that you have for Jesus Christ is in your heart…that then provides an attitude and an atmosphere in the home which is conducive for a child learning and growing and living the faith.

Anne Graham Lotz, the daughter of Billy and Ruth Graham, is a wonderful Bible teacher and Christian speaker. She loves the Word of God. And she was asked, "When did you develop such a love for God's Word?" Naturally, you would think she would have mentioned her father's sermons, but she didn't. She said, "I developed the love of God's Word when, as a little girl, I would walk by my mother's room and see her with her Bible open, with commentaries of Scripture all around, and she would be pouring over the Scriptures. She loved the Scriptures. And because of my mother's devotion and dedication to the Word of God, a desire was implanted in me to know and to love God's Word as well."

Like Anne, your kids need the right example!

By the way, the word *teach* in Deuteronomy 6:7 means to

sharpen. It speaks of a penetrating stab…a deep cut. It's not just rules and regulations…external lists or rigid dogmatism. It's reaching deeply into the soul of your child.

Josh McDowell says, "Rules without a relationship equals rebellion." In other words, if all you have are rules without the loving relationship and environment of family, it can produce rebellion in the heart of your child. Children not only need principles taught to them, they need those principles lived out before them. And they need explanations. Not just, "Because I said so," but rather, "Because God leads us so." You may want to ask yourself the simplest of all questions: "What kind of Christian would my child be if my child were just like me?" As Andrew Murray said, "The secret of home rule is self rule."

Training Your Child

One of the most-quoted verses related to parenting is Proverbs 22:6. This verse tells us:

Train up a child in the way he should go; even when he is old he will not depart from it.

While this is a wonderful promise, it is primarily a precept for parents in how they raise their children. In fact, the word *child* in this verse describes the formative, developmental years of the child. Let me help you understand what this verse is really saying…and how it can impact the way you raise your child.

First is the phrase *train up*. This really is an intriguing phrase. This phrase was used in the ancient world when a midwife would take a newborn infant and cleanse its mouth, creating a thirst and a hunger for food. Training up a child is to create a hunger and a thirst for the things of God.

But this phrase was also used to describe the breaking of a horse…bringing a horse into submission. So not only does training your child mean creating a thirst for the things of God, it also means bringing a child into submission and helping him or her deal with the natural rebellion that's found in all of us.

Second, we need to understand that no two children are the same. Some are compliant, some are defiant. Every child is different. Like the snowflake. The parent who is wise knows that no two children are alike. That's why the Scripture says that we are to train up our children "in the way he should go."

Some translations render that phrase as, "according to his own bent or inclination." So it's not about fitting your child into your mold, but rather, raising your child according to the basic temperament and personality and giftedness of that particular child.

And if you are going to do this, it takes time. You have to study your child, know your child, look into his or her eyes, hold them close, and spend enough time with them to make wise decisions on how to raise them according to who they are.

Third, we need to understand what it means when it says, "when he is old." The word for *old* actually means when he gets hair on his chin...which refers primarily to a boy becoming a young man or a girl becoming a young woman. If we will do our job as parents, God says, "I'll do My job and I will work in the heart of your child."

Think of the tremendous potential your child has. Every child is made with the possibility...the potential...of being restored to the image of Jesus Christ. Each was formed and framed by the hand of God. Jeremiah said, "I was called to be a prophet in my mother's womb." David, describing the birth process in Psalm 139, spoke of being knitted in his mother's womb, created by the hand of God.

But with the great possibilities of every child, there are problems. In Psalm 51:5, David says, "In sin did my mother conceive me." He's not saying that the act of conception is sin, but rather, he was born with a sinful nature. In fact, David later says in the Psalms that children come forth from their mother's womb speaking lies. That's why you don't have to teach your little darling to lie...and why you have to teach your child *not* to lie. And why you don't have to teach a child to steal, but you have to teach him or her *not* to steal.

There is rebellion in the heart of a child. And that's why a child needs to come to know Jesus Christ as Lord and Savior and the forgiveness of sin as soon as possible in their young lives.

So let's put it all together: A child is a gift from God, created by God and given to us as a stewardship to nurture. And it is our responsibility as parents to direct our children and lead them to faith in Jesus Christ.

Disciplining Your Children

One final area I want to touch on is the discipline of your children. I believe that Psalm 127:4 not only speaks of direction, it also speaks of discipline. In your hands as a parent is the responsibility to help your children be disciplined. If you don't discipline your children, somebody else will discipline them for you.

In the 1960s, Dr. Spock popularized the notion that kids should not be spanked. And we had a generation of kids who were raised on Spock instead of spank!

Why is it important to discipline a child? Proverbs 22:15 tells us, "Folly is bound up in the heart of a child, but the rod of discipline drives it far from him."

It's natural for a child to make foolish decisions and foolish choices, so it's vital you start disciplining them when they are young. If you start disciplining your children early... and I mean a little spank every now and then...it will save you a lot of heartache and anxiety later on.

Yes, spanking is okay—if it's done properly. Obviously, I'm not talking about the angry, abusive beating of children, which is absolutely wrong. Any person who abuses a child in that manner is not worthy to be a parent! I'm talking about an appropriate pop on the seat of learning!

God has given every child a spanking place. It's made just for that! In fact, a child ought to be raised with two pats on the back...one high enough to let them know they've done well and one low enough to correct them when they've done wrong.

But let me warn you: Never punish a child when you're angry. Slow down...and wait before you do it. Be patient, loving, and kind, and correct your child to remove foolishness. As Proverbs 23:13-14 says:

Do not withhold discipline from a child; if you strike him with a rod, he will not die. If you strike him with the rod, you will save his soul from Sheol.

Yes, your child may *think* he's dying when he or she is disciplined. But if you love your child enough to discipline them, you will redirect them and help save them from a life that is truly destructive. Proverbs 29:15 tells us, "The rod and reproof give wisdom, but a child left to himself brings shame to his mother."

And we have plenty of children left to themselves today, don't we? They're called latch-key kids…kids who let themselves in after school and learn their morals from MTV. They used to be raised at their mother's knee, but now they're raised by the media!

As a result, kids are joining the wrong crowd. They're looking for a family…some place where they are loved and where they feel like they belong! Children left to themselves bring sorrow, but when they're corrected, they gain wisdom.

I've heard parents say, "I just love my little darling too much to spank them." Really? What parents are really saying is that they don't love their child enough to risk their displeasure. As Scripture tells us, "For the Lord disciplines the one He loves, and chastises every son whom He receives" (Hebrews 12:6). If you love your child, you will discipline him!

But when you discipline your children, you need to explain why you are disciplining them…and when it's over, warmly embrace them and tell them you love them.

You never want to break a child's spirit—that's called exasperating a child. But you do want to help the child's will to be broken and submitted to God. You want to make sure that his or her little heart becomes tender to the Lord…and responsive and respectful to you.

If you're anything like me, you have to admit that you've failed many times as a parent. But you know something? Our kids aren't looking for perfect parents. But they are expecting us to be consistent in what we say, what we believe, and how we live our lives. Remember that little ears are listening to what you say, and little eyes are watching what you do!

So how are you doing as a parent today? If you need to make some adjustments, ask God to help you. Ask Him to help you rearrange your lifestyle to make whatever sacrifices are necessary. It may even mean downscaling. Whatever it is, commit yourself and your children to the Lord. If you do, one day you will say…as John the apostle said…"I have no greater joy than to hear that my children are walking in the truth" (3 John 1:4).

CHAPTER 5

Protecting Your Marriage

Whenever I watch a sporting event, I love to watch the offense play. The offense is exciting because it leads to scoring points and when that happens, the crowd goes crazy! But you know what? Without defense, the offense can't do their job.

In most sports, defensive players don't get a lot of recognition. Defense is just tough! It's a lot of hard work down in the trenches, and it's not really that glamorous.

But defense is vital if a team is going to win. And defending and protecting your marriage is vital if you are going to keep your marriage strong. It's like doing preventative maintenance on your car. From time to time, you have to take your automobile in to have it serviced. And it's the same with your marriage. You need to have a "service plan" to keep your marriage running strong.

My friend and personal physician, Dr. Ken Cooper, talks

a great deal about preventative medicine. With proper rest, exercise, diet, and regular checkups, we can protect ourselves and prevent problems before they have a chance to become more significant.

The same is true in marriage. 1 Peter 5:8 warns us, "Your adversary the devil prowls around like a roaring lion, seeking someone to devour." So we must do everything we can to prevent the destruction and the demise of our marriage…our home…and our family!

In Luke 6:46-49, we find the words of Jesus at the close of the Sermon on the Mount. This is what He says:

"Why do you call me 'Lord, Lord,' and not do what I tell you? Everyone who comes to me and hears my words and does them, I will show you what he is like: he is like a man building a house, who dug deep and laid the foundation on the rock. And when a flood arose, the stream broke against that house and could not shake it, because it had been well built. But the one who hears and does not do them is like a man who built a house on the ground without a foundation.

When the stream broke against it, immediately it fell,

and the ruin of that house was great. "

What a description of the American family today! The ruin of the households in America is great and the reverberations in the lives of our children and future generations are truly significant. The brokenness is everywhere. When you have broken hearts, you have broken homes...and when you have broken homes, you have broken humans.

The purpose of this chapter is to raise a standard...to challenge you to never walk away from your marriage. To take the measures necessary to protect your marriage...and your family.

Now, you may be in a situation where your marriage has already fallen apart. If so, you need to know that the grace of God is sufficient to give you a brand new beginning in Jesus Christ. Affirm that, celebrate that, and rejoice in that!

But we also need to recognize that according to Malachi 2:16, God hates divorce. And in Mark 10:9, Jesus said, "What therefore God has joined together, let not man separate." God makes it clear that we have a responsibility to commit ourselves to our marriage throughout our lives. And this means loving your mate enough to protect the commitment you made to each other.

Marry Right

Now, the natural question is, "How do I protect my marriage so that it lasts a lifetime?"

First of all, as followers of Christ, we should be spiritually compatible with our mate. That's the only way we can work together as a team to accomplish the goals that God has given us. The Scripture is very clear on this subject. We should marry a person who shares our faith and spiritual commitment. Paul tells us in 2 Corinthians 6:14 that we are not to be unequally yoked with unbelievers. *Period!*

You are not smarter than God. And you need to recognize that the most important part of you is the part that is made for God. And in order for you to be compatible with another person, you must be spiritually compatible. This means you must marry someone who knows and loves the Lord Jesus Christ and who is willing to walk in obedience to Him.

If a person loves Jesus like that, he or she will love you more than is humanly possible. And if you marry a child of the devil, it won't be long till you'll start having trouble with your father-in-law. And the devil isn't someone you want to have for a father-in-law!

So it's vitally important that you commit yourself to Jesus Christ and that you find a mate who shares that spiritual conviction and commitment.

Amos 3:3 says, "Do two walk together, unless they have agreed to meet?" If you marry someone who doesn't share your spiritual faith and commitment in Christ, you will always have points of contention that are difficult to solve.

As a believer, you will want to tithe your income and sacrificially give to the work of Jesus Christ. But your mate will resist you on that. Or you will want to pray about a problem in your home or your marriage. But your unbelieving mate won't want to pray about it, but rather, he or she will just want to "work things out." You'll want to go to church, but your mate will say that it's their day off and they don't want to waste their time at church.

Or you will want to raise your children in the nurture and the admonition of the Lord. But your unbelieving mate will not want to "push religion down your kids' throats."

There will be a spiritual division...a division in the most important part of your life, which is your commitment to Jesus Christ. So the first step in protecting your marriage is to not marry someone outside the faith. And if you do, and you're not careful, spiritual decay will settle into your own life.

This means that if you are single, you should never date someone who you would not marry. Because if you begin to date someone and you allow a love to grow in your heart for that person, it will be very, very difficult for you to let go. My admonition to you is this: Instead of looking for a mate, start asking God to make you the person He wants you to be. Ultimately...in His own perfect will and timing...He will lead you to the right person.

Pay the Price

Once you have honored God by marrying someone who is a fellow believer, you must be willing to pay the price of commitment. And commitment takes diligence and hard work.

Don't assume that your marriage won't have any problems. It will. In fact, when I counsel couples with marital problems, most of them say something like this: "We never dreamed this could happen to us. We never imagined we would be here in this situation."

Pastor and author Alistair Begg reminds us that marriage is like a garden that must be tended. If you neglect the garden, what happens? Weeds and pests of all kinds get in.

A healthy garden needs tending. And a healthy garden needs lots of water. If you are to protect your marriage, you must refresh your marriage with the water of the Word of God, making the Scripture a part of your life.

That's what Jesus is talking about in Luke 6. He is challenging you to build your life, your marriage, and your house on the Rock, which is Him and His Word.

So many marriages are in trouble today because husbands and wives just don't know what God's Word says. You have to be willing to pay the price…and it starts by committing yourself and your marriage to be built on the truth of God's

Word...which is THE marriage manual.

But even if you commit to build your marriage on the Rock of Jesus Christ and His Word, it's still possible for your marriage to struggle if you aren't diligently working at it. In fact, most marriages don't blow out. They fizzle out. How does this happen? The sizzle is replaced with a fizzle because you aren't taking care of business. You aren't working at it. You're not *practicing* the Word of God in your life and in your marriage.

Today, if the light is flickering in your marriage, you need to do everything you can to fight for it and for your future together. Don't give up! Don't quit! Be willing to sacrifice and to work at it diligently. A great marriage takes hard work!

You know, the opposite of love isn't hate, it's indifference or apathy. It says, "I don't care." Many marriages fall apart because of apathy—not because of hatred, bitterness, or rancor. They fall apart because the husband or wife...or both...just don't care anymore.

If that's where you find yourself today, I challenge you to ask God to renew your spirit, rekindle your love, and give you the hope that is in Jesus Christ to keep working at it.

It's Never Too Late

No matter where you might find your marriage today, I want you to know that it's never too late. So don't ever give up!

In Luke 6, Jesus talks about storms coming against both houses. And that's so true. Storms do come in life and in marriage, even if you've built your marriage on the Rock of Jesus Christ. There are all kinds of assaults and winds that blow against our marriages today. In fact, it seems that everything in our culture today works against the lifestyle of the Christian marriage, home, and family.

When I think about the challenges a Christian marriage faces and the storms that come against it, I think about a man named Noah. God told him how he could be rescued from the storm that was going to engulf the earth by building a boat…a boat that would be big enough for his family and all those animals. And Noah, in obedience, did exactly what God told him to do.

The day came when God said, "Gather your family and the animals and get in the boat. And stay in that boat till the storm is over." And that's exactly what Noah did. He got in the boat and he stayed in it. No matter how rough the seas became, he stayed in that boat. And if he hadn't obeyed...if one day he had decided to get out of the boat, he and his family would have drowned. They would have died. They would have gone under.

But Noah did exactly what God told him to do, no matter how rough it was...no matter how hard it rained and poured... no matter how smelly those stinking animals were in that ark. Noah and his family stayed in the boat!

And that's what I'm challenging you to do. No matter how tough it is...no matter how stormy it is...no matter how difficult the struggles might be that your marriage faces...stay in the boat! Stay strong in the Lord Jesus Christ and keep the commitment you have made to your marriage.

Now, there are two typical responses I hear from people who are wanting to bail out on their marriages.

One is, **"I'm not happy."**

That's the perspective of the world today! We live in a culture that's most interested in self-advancement and absorbed in self-preoccupation. As a result, we easily abandon commitments because we believe we deserve to be happy in life.

Let me remind you: As a believer, God's primary purpose is not to make you happy. It's to make you holy. And the way to be holy is to be obedient to Jesus Christ and His Word. Remember what Jesus said in Luke 6:46: "Why do you call me 'Lord, Lord,' and not do what I tell you?"

You are to obey Him...which means you should never give up on your marriage...even if you aren't happy.

The second thing I often hear is, **"I don't love my spouse anymore."**

You can always learn to love someone, especially since you have the Spirit of the Living God...the Spirit of Jesus Christ...who is incarnate love, living in you. You possess the power of the greatest love in the history of the world. And through that love, you can by God's grace learn to love again. I've seen God rekindle and restore marriages that I felt were humanly beyond help. So I know God can change your heart and He can give you the love you need for your spouse!

In Revelation 2:4, Jesus said to a backslidden church, "You have abandoned the love you had at first." Note that He didn't say, "You have *lost* the love you had at first." He said, "You have *abandoned* the love you had at first." Then what did He say? Jesus said, "Repent, and do the works you did at first." In other words, return to what you used to do when you loved Me the most...when you loved Me the best. Start doing what you did then, and before long, the first love will be back again.

And the same principle applies in marriage. Sometimes you have to start all over!

So, if you sense that the love in your marriage is ebbing, I encourage you to return, go back, and start over today! Begin to rebuild your marriage. Do whatever it takes...even if you feel like your marriage is beyond repair! Remember, the Bible says, "I can do all things through Him who strengthens me" (Philippians 4:13). So don't give up. It's never too late.

Learn to Sacrifice

Once you've committed to not give up on your marriage, you need to be willing to make whatever sacrifice that is necessary to keep it strong and healthy.

As we noted earlier, husbands and wives are to commit themselves in mutual submission to one another. This will probably take some sacrifice, but your marriage should be typified by you giving of yourself to your mate...not you taking whatever you can get and then bailing out.

Christian writer and counselor Dennis Rainey tells the story of Dr. Robertson McQuilkin and his wife, Muriel. Dr. and Mrs. McQuilkin were a dynamic ministry team. Dr. McQuilkin was the president of Columbia Bible College and Seminary and Mrs. McQuilkin had her own local radio talk show.

After many years of marriage, Muriel's health began to deteriorate, and eventually tests confirmed that she had Alzheimer's disease. And over the next few years, Muriel began to lose many of her basic motor skills. She couldn't speak clearly and she was unable to think clearly. Before long, she couldn't feed, bathe, or take care of herself.

As the president of a Christian institution, Dr. McQuilkin faced a difficult decision: Should he put his wife in an institution where she could be cared for or quit his job to take care of Muriel full time? After all, he was called to be the president of this wonderful Christian organization…and God was blessing that work.

Here is what Dr. McQuilkin wrote in *Christianity Today*: "When the time came, the decision was firm. It took no great calculation. It was a matter of integrity. Had I not promised 42 years before 'in sickness and in health, to love, honor, and cherish as long as we both shall live'? This was no grim duty to which I was stoically resigned, however. It was only fair. She had, after all, cared for me almost for four decades with marvelous devotion. Now it was my turn. And such a partner she was, my Muriel. If I took care of her for 40 years, I would never be out of her debt."

And so, Dr. McQuilkin resigned his position to take care of his beloved Muriel full time.

Now, the question is, are you willing to do whatever it

takes...to sacrifice in order to keep the commitment that you made to your spouse? Are you committed to do what you said you would do? Remember, your marriage is not a mere human contract that can be torn up and put in file 13. It's a divine contract containing sacred vows and promises that you made to God and to each other.

So what sacrifices are you willing to make in order for God to be honored and glorified and for your marriage, home, and family to be blessed?

That commitment begins in your heart. If you have broken your commitment...if you have gone your own way...repent and ask God in your brokenness to rebuild your life and rebuild your marriage. And determine by God's grace and by the help of Jesus Christ, that you will be committed together as long as you both shall live.

Build your house upon Jesus Christ. Build your life upon Him and you will never, never regret it.

CHAPTER 6

Passing the Torch

"**B**ut as for me and my house, we will serve the LORD" (Joshua 24:15).

The family is under assault today. There are forces at work that are tearing families apart…forces that are tempting you to compromise, to choose a course that can mean heartache and pain.

In these 12 words from Joshua 24, we find the key to keeping our families together in this day and age. We find the secret to successfully passing the torch on to future generations. These are the words of Joshua when he made a commitment to the Lord God and to his family. It was a decided, deliberate, and determined commitment to pass the torch of living for God on to his children.

Before he died, Joshua gathered the children of Israel together and gave them an appeal that is recorded for us in Joshua 23 and 24. In this appeal, Joshua warns the generations to come about the dangers of compromise. He challenges them to understand the importance of choosing right over wrong. And he invites them to respond in faith, hope, and happiness… and to follow the Lord God fully.

As he comes to the end of his address, Joshua simply lets the children of Israel know that he doesn't know what path they may choose, but "as for me and my house, we will serve the LORD."

Joshua leaves no room for neutrality…no room for equivocation. This was fearless, faithful leadership from a man who loved God and wanted his family and the future generations of Israel to love God and to serve Him with all their hearts.

It's been suggested in sociological circles that children and teenagers in the 1950s lost their innocence. While it was a time of "Happy Days," there was a price. That price was the loss of innocence.

And then in the '60s, American youth lost their respect for authority. From the war in Vietnam to the crises in the hearts and lives of students and young adults, there was a rebellion that shook the core of our country. And the children of the '60s lost respect for authority.

In the '70s, we're told that a generation lost their love. It became the "me" generation, with sex becoming a substitute for real love. And the "What's in it for me?" world became the ideal and the goal of many.

We still see the impact of the '50s, '60s, and '70s. And today, we have a generation that has lost hope. That's why teenage suicides are at an all time high. That's why so many kids today are walking around in a fog, wondering what life is all about. We have a generation of kids who are on a downward spiral with the driving question being, "When and how is it going to stop?"

It's only going to stop if a new generation of men and women called of God will stand strong and firm like Joshua and say, "Regardless of what anybody else does...regardless of what the world may do...'as for me and my house, we will serve the LORD.'"

So what are we talking about when we commit to have our families serve the Lord?

There are five goals I want to give you for your children. If you seek to make these your goals, you will have a family that, like Joshua's, is committed to serve the Lord...and can withstand the storms of this generation.

Confident Children

The first goal for a family that's dedicated to serving the Lord is to produce confident children. Confident, optimistic, happy children know who they are...and especially know who they are in Jesus Christ.

When I used to drop my kids off at school or at a birthday party, I'd say something like this from time to time: "Remember who you are and whose you are." I wasn't reminding them that they belonged to me. I was reminding them that they belonged to God.

As parents, our goal must be to raise children who are confident in Christ and who have a life that is filled with love, hope, and dreams for the future. These are confident children.

Children of Conviction

Second, we must raise children of conviction. And when I talk about conviction, I'm talking about beliefs.

In the battle for the soul of this nation, the battleground is the home and the issue is truth…which is anchored in authority, values, and what we believe.

Satan, the master deceiver, is actively misleading our kids. He's feeding thousands upon thousands of lies into their minds and attacking the very foundations of our homes. And the psalmist says, "If the foundations are destroyed, what can the righteous do?" (Psalm 11:3).

Polls indicate that the majority of Americans do not believe in absolute truth. And this includes many who claim to be followers of Christ! As a result of this lack of conviction, we have a generation that is morally adrift and without direction.

Let me remind you that God has given us truth in the person of Jesus Christ. And He has given us truth in the Word of God. Mom and Dad, it's your responsibility to teach your children truth. Convictional truth.

I challenge you to help your kids to grow up with more

than opinions or preferences. Help them grow up with convictions that come from the Word of God. Not truths that are practiced when it's convenient. Not truths that are practiced when it's comfortable. And not cultural truths that change with the times! But convictional truth that comes from God.

Children of Character

The third goal should be to produce children of character. Now, truth transforms character. There really is no ultimate character without the conviction that comes from knowing the truth.

Rules without convictions only produce potential phonies and hypocrites. If all you instill in your child are behaviors through your rules, as soon as they're out of the house...at the party, away for the weekend, or off to college on their own... they're going to be one thing in the world and one thing when they are at home.

That's why character starts with conviction. It's not formed by just saying, "Do this because I say so." Character is formed when a child understands, "This is what God says," which is revealed through the truth of Scripture. You need to help your child embrace the values taught in the Word of God. That truth will transform the inner life and the inner character of your child, which will produce a person of integrity. Your child will then know the difference between right and wrong... and will be courageous enough to stand for truth, regardless of their situation.

Children of Compassion

Fourth, I challenge you to produce children of compassion. Kids today have a sense of entitlement. These kids are looking for the next handout that they believe they deserve.

I'm afraid that we've given our kids so many things that we have a generation that is extremely self-focused, constantly looking for someone to give them something. We need to turn that around and produce a generation of children who care...who think first of others...who live lives of love and compassion.

I've seen this kind of transformation take place as the young people in my church have gone to the mission field,

picked up little children that are hurting, and loved them…
expressing and sharing the Gospel of Jesus Christ. In doing
so, they've turned from the cult of self-importance to be people
of compassion.

You know, I'll never forget the time I saw my daughter
as a high school student pick up a small, underprivileged child
and tell her about Jesus. I was overwhelmed because I realized
that this is what it's about…our children walking in truth and
sharing the truth of Jesus Christ with others.

So seek to raise children of compassion…kids who don't
just rise to the top and make a lot of money, but kids who make
a difference in the world for Jesus Christ!

Children of Competence

Another quality I challenge you to build into your child is
competence. What do I mean by that? That your children will
live responsible lives—that they will be equipped, endowed,
and encouraged with the gifts and the abilities that God has
given them to make a difference in the world. If you raise
competent children, they will become competent adults who

then one day will be mature parents who will keep passing the torch to the next generation.

When you think about all this, it can be overwhelming, can't it? We've all messed up as parents, and it can be overwhelming when you think of the responsibilities we have.

But remember what the Bible says: "I can do all things through Him who strengthens me" (Philippians 4:13). You can do this through the power and presence of Christ in your life one day at a time! So don't shrink back. Instead, stand firm *today* and do all you can to build into your children a competence that will serve them for life.

Bill Hybels has said, Christian parents who truly understand the goal of parenting become fully engaged in the challenge. They no longer just build businesses: They build character, value and vision into young lives. They no longer treat their children as an inconvenience to be handed off to anyone who will tend to them for $5.00 an hour. These parents see the season of parenting as the ultimate spiritual challenge, worthy of their best efforts, most

fervent prayers and largest investments of time.
They search for ways to improve their skills through
books and tapes and seminars and interacting with
other parents. These parents look to the church for
assistance and they support with their time, money
and prayer the ministries that enhance their children's
spiritual training. In short, they do anything that they
can do to encourage authentic, Christian growth
in their children, even if it slows their professional
advancement and postpones the pursuit of personal
dreams. They know that molding a runny-nosed little
bandit into a God-honoring difference-maker is the
most stretching, demanding, and ultimately fulfilling
challenge they can face.

My prayer for you is that you will be that kind of parent!
But to do so, you must be engaged with your children.

Notice that Joshua 24:15 is plural: "As for me and
my house, *we* will serve the LORD" (italics added). Too
many parents want to have children, but they don't make a
commitment to raise those children. Every couple knows what

it takes to conceive children, but not many are willing to make the commitment to raise those children. Apparently, some parents think children raise themselves!

Your children require your active participation, interest, and involvement. As a pastor for over 30 years, I've observed that the best kids are kids who are raised in families where their parents are involved actively and aggressively in their lives. While there are exceptions, I've seen the impact parents have when they're involved in the lives of their kids.

Too many young people today wonder if their parents really care. It's like this letter from a teenager to his mom and dad:

Dear Mom and Dad,

I don't think I've ever written you a letter, but I am now, because I know if I tried to say these things to you, you wouldn't have the time to listen. It's just that ever since I turned 13, something terrible has happened to us. We used to have fun together. Now all you do is yell at me about something...my room, my hair, my clothes, my stereo, my TV, my friends, my grades. It's like whatever I do makes you mad.

I know I screw up, but Mom and Dad, what's killing me inside is that since you seem so mad all the time, I don't want to be around you anymore. I know it's not cool to want to be around your parents, but I'm so lonely. I've got lots of friends. School is okay and football is great, but I've got all this stuff inside me and I've got all these questions about life and myself and God. Oh, I talk to my friends about girls and parties and football, but I can't tell my friends, "Gee, guys, I'm lonely." I'm actually afraid...afraid of relationships with girls and the pressure to have sex. When I'm alone (and I'm alone more than you think), I just fill my time with music, friends, and TV. But it doesn't do any good and I'm still lonely and scared.

So here I am...a senior in high school feeling like a stranger in my own family. I look so together to everyone out there, but inside I'm dying. I'm so afraid I will leave home and go to college and get married and end up like both of you...strangers to each other

and strangers to my own children.

I'm afraid to give this letter to you because I'm afraid you'll get mad, or worse, you'll just ignore it. I don't think I can stand any more rejection. Actually, I don't know if I'll ever give this letter to you.

Now more than ever, your kids need your involvement and your presence in their lives. And if you don't know how to spell the word *presence*, it's spelled *T-I-M-E*. And there's no substitute for it. God never intended for children to be raised by babysitters, nannies, schoolteachers, daycare workers, or relatives. God will hold us accountable for the stewardship of our children.

Now, if you're a single parent, I salute you. You bear the weight and responsibility of both parents with incredible financial burdens, and you have very few options. And I know many single parents who are making it against all odds. So I'm not talking to you, as I understand your situation.

But I am talking to couples who like having children but don't like taking care of them. It's time to stop and reevaluate your priorities and your lifestyle if you are not giving time to your kids!

I believe we have more discretionary time than our parents, and yet, many parents are using their discretionary times for themselves. You can't microwave children into maturity. It takes effort and energy…and lots of it! The problem in our society today, as far as I'm concerned, is not delinquent kids, but drop-out dads and misguided moms who have their priorities all out of whack.

I was scared when I went into the ministry because I had seen a lot of preachers before me who lost their kids. The words of Jesus echoed, "For what does it profit a man to gain the whole world and forfeit his life?" (Mark 8:36). What does it profit a Christian and a minister if he wins the whole world and loses his own family?

So I made some decisions early on about the time I would spend with my kids. I knew I had to if my goal and my passion was for my children, grandchildren, and great-grandchildren to love Jesus Christ and serve Him.

The Scripture gives us a promise when it says, "The

generation of the upright will be blessed" (Psalm 112:2). If we want our descendents to be blessed and see our children's children serving and loving and honoring Jesus Christ, then we ought to be praying, "Oh, God, start a fire in me that will never be put out. Start it in my family."

I love what Paul said to young Timothy in 2 Timothy 1:5: "I am reminded of your sincere faith, a faith that dwelt first in your grandmother Lois and your mother Eunice and now, I am sure, dwells in you as well." For all we know, Eunice and Lois were single parents. Or maybe they were married to men who didn't know Christ. But in Timothy's case, the faith was passed on from his grandmother to his mother to Timothy. It was a legacy of faith that started with his grandmother.

Most grandparents have no clue how important they are to the lives of their grandchildren. What is a grandma? This is how a third-grader thinks about a grandma:

A grandma is a lady who has no kids of her own
so she likes other people's little girls and boys. A
grandfather is a man-grandmother. He goes for walks,
and they talk about fishing and tractors and stuff like

that. Grandmothers don't have to do anything but just be there. They're so old they shouldn't play or run. It's enough just to drive us to the market so we can ride the pretend horses and have lots of money ready. When they take us for walks, they slow down past the pretty things and we look at leaves and caterpillars. They never say, "Hurry up." Usually they are fat, but not too fat to tie their shoes. They wear glasses and funny underwear and they take their teeth and gums out at night when they go to bed. They don't have to be smart, except to answer questions like: Why do dogs hate cats? and, How come God isn't married? When they read to us, they don't skip. And they don't mind if it's the same story over and over again. Everybody should try to have one...especially if you don't have a TV, because grandmas have a lot of time.

Timothy's faith began in the heart of his grandmother. And many of us today bear the torch of truth handed on to us from generations before. Now it's our turn...our time to pass it along.

We must be committed to future generations. When Joshua said, "As for me and my house, *we* will serve the LORD," he was passing along his faith to his family… and beyond.

You and I are to raise our children not to bear our name, but to bear the name of Jesus Christ. That's why God gave us those kids…to be lights in the world…to be lights in dark places…to be witnesses in a place and a time we will never see. We must see it as our responsibility to take the torch of truth and pass it along to our kids. Not to make a name for ourselves, but to make a name for the Lord our God.

A while back, my brother and I returned home to attend the funeral service of one of our uncles who had passed away. It ended up being a "Roots" tour, and many memories flooded my heart.

One of those memories was of my grandfather who, as a godly Sunday school teacher and deacon, would put me on his knee every night and teach the Scriptures to me. And I can tell you that the torch of truth was passed to me…a light was lit in my heart as a little towheaded boy in Arkansas. And by God's grace, Deb and I are passing it on to our kids and grandkids.

One day, when our family is gathered around the Throne of Grace, my greatest joy will be to report, "Lord, we're all here. We're here together. And look, here are the generations, one after another, Lord, following You."

I pray the same will be true for you. That you will pass the torch to your children…and in doing so, impact future generations until Jesus comes again. ◆